SUN FLOWER INK
Palo Colorado Canyon, Carmel, Calif. 93923

Even
As We Speak

by RIC MASTEN

ACKNOWLEDGMENTS

All of the poems in Section II SUNFLOWERS originally appeared in booklet form published in 1971 by the *Unitarian Universalist Association.* Second printing 1972. Third printing 1975. Fourth printing 1976. A revised paperback edition was published by *Palo Colorado Press* in 1978. Second printing 1979.

The song lyrics are published by *Mastensville Music Publishing* licensed through *Broadcast Music, Inc.*

Cover painting and sketches by Gary Rusk.

Photographs on back cover by David Darby Ray.

NICHOLS & DIMES

The book was produced by NICHOLS & DIMES, 1025 West 15th Street, Odessa, Texas. 79763.

(paperback) 9 8 7 6 5 4 3 2 1

Library of congress Catalogue Card No. 82-60705
ISBN 0-931104-12-2

FOR SWEET BILLIE
OF THE TELEPHONE BOOTH

Contents

II SUNFLOWERS

III SUNFLOWER SEEDS

BACKWORDS

Foreword

Why am I writing a "foreword" about Ric Masten's poetry, when you, the reader, should be experiencing the poetry directly? Most people read the "foreword" last anyway, but here I am wandering through Big Sur country, through Ric Masten's magic mountain home, and through his life for the moment, and he asked me to speak with you. It is difficult to "speak" with you in print, especially for me, a philosopher-language-teacher, who likes to enter into dialogue with others. The word "speak" itself is a spoken utterance, not just a printed medium. Struggling with the first poem (or last poem, depending on how you read the book) in this collection, any words that I write are my perceptions frozen in print. In the title poem, EVEN AS WE SPEAK, I need the "we" in order to enter into a dialogue — the other voices that share experiences, emotions, perceptions, making the words, the poems, become alive. I also need the recognition of time, that even as I write, the moment slips away. There are no "even" moments. One moment of time/experience gives rise to the next one. It is only in the reflecting consciousness that we can look back at our lives in progress.

EVEN AS WE SPEAK is a collection of poems that attempts to capture the life-history moment of Ric Masten, as he now exists in 1982, looking backward to his commercial songs in 1958. I wish there could be the definitive edition, a collection of the Works of Ric Masten, but then, Ric would be dead; and even as we are speaking to one another, Ric is upstairs changing, writing another poem for the continuation of the dialogue. The reader should remember to read the book backwards, just as your life begins with the here-and-now, revisioning your life from its own turning point. As you notice Ric Masten's poetry in the first section, WEEDS (written since 1980), you will share the problems of a fatigued problem-solver; in the second section, SUNFLOWERS (first published in 1971, not out of print and unavailable), you will experience those human problems that bring us pain, sorrow, and grief; and in section three, SUNFLOWER SEEDS, you will reach back to the 1960's for a few hard protest pieces, experiencing the struggle between protest and profit; finally, you can conclude the entire collection with a couple of popular, commercial song lyrics Ric wrote in Hollywood, while he was pumping gas with a pen, finding yourself at the beginning of the poet's ever-changing life/work. In any case, remember that each moment of pain, suffering, anger, despair, protest, grief, and humor is only one side of a life. It is the dialogue between poet and audience that opens the threshold of hope, that allows us to cry together, yet laugh together, "bearing" the journey of the life-moment. Anybody who does not see the humor as well as the serious side in the poetry is already dead and is not reading this foreword anyway.

If you do not, at this time, wish to hear my views on Ric Masten and his poetry, then go directly to the poems themselves. If you are the type of reader that demands an explanation, an analysis, the "meaning," before you read the poetry, then go to the back section of the book *(Backwords)* and read the critical analysis by Robert O'Brien, a Professor of Philosophy; or a personal look at Ric's "Wizardry" by Dr. Roberta Richards, Psychologist; or an exploration of Ric's learning disabilities by G. Lynn Nelson, English Education Instructor. But remember these other voices, including my own, are people who have been sparked by the poems of Ric Masten and by the interaction with the person in dialogue; and even as we speak, there could be many interpretations; and the best ones should be yours.

Each of us has his/her own unique statement to make in life. After we pay our dues—sorrow, grief, anger, protest, fatigue, struggle—we are revitalized with hope, courage, honesty, and communion/bonding with the other voices— friends, parents, lovers, teachers. In a world of dehumaniza- tion, it is the poet who accepts the entire struggle for becoming human, the focal point for our inability to put into words the paradoxes, the humor, and the dead seriousness of the world in which we live. Ric Masten's poetry is a "nexus," a web or net that captures our experiences, yet allows the emotional flow of life to continue. We are receptive, open to the poetry, like antennas receiving signals in the "electric air" in order to find ways to get to the next moment in life, a "crossing," metaphors for experience. But the poet never gives you a pat answer, because you are engaged in the search for yourself, even as we speak, even as you read his poetry. These experiences, captured in the poet's net, are sometimes painful, yet somehow uplifting, allowing us to continue life's journey. Ric Masten's poetry might appear at times to be a "downer," but there is always some hidden hope that needs to be unveiled by the interaction between you, the audience, and the poet's words.

Who, then, is Ric Masten? Even as we speak, he has changed. I have known him over ten years and he still surprises me, depresses me, lifts me, makes me think /feel/be/do, and, most of all, makes me laugh. But, by my own observations of Ric, on the road, in my classes, in my home, and in his home, I can say at least this much about him: RIC MASTEN IS A POET OF THE MIND. He literally speaks his mind through his poetry, and he is not afraid to change his mind. Over the years his work reflects different positions and opinions about his struggles, protests, and discoveries. Often, he protests the protest that he first believed. It is this open mind that expresses sincerity and authenticity. By no means is he abstract or too "heavy" for his audiences, hiding behind jargon or terminology, yet he is truly Everyman's philosopher.

RIC MASTEN IS A POET OF THE SENSES. At times, he uses techniques similar to Rilke's "mixed association of the senses"; at other times, he uses "common sense." It is this direct appeal to the common-sense person that allows Ric Masten to reach many various, unique audiences. What appears at first to be simple becomes a complexity of associations in our muddled lives. He is truly a poet of democracy.

RIC MASTEN IS A POET OF THE BODY. In a peculiar fashion, the poetry reveals a certain time and age that each of us experiences in our own unique way: the child, exploring the wonder and myths about life; the young, virile rebel searching for truths; the middle-age crazy, sorting out the bombardment of the experiences, and the wise, older wizard, looking back at life as a dance. Ric Masten's poetry appeals to all ages for this reason. I have seen him with children, who cannot hold their bodies still, but do; with senior citizens, who are slowly losing their bodies; and even with prisoners, whose bodies are locked up.

RIC MASTEN IS A POET OF THE HEART. The emotional bond between audience and poet is the essence of the poet's works. Ric Masten wants his poetry to spark the emotional center of our being. Recognition and acceptance of our confused emotional tribulations in life allows the bonding between humans, the communion of those on the threshold of hope.

RIC MASTEN IS A POET OF THE SOUL. Here is poetry that can be accepted by the sacred as well as by the secular worshipper. Ric Masten uses religious symbols and allegories from different religions and sometimes even questions the misunderstanding and deception about the process of becoming religious. He takes us through the dark night of the soul to the light of self-sufficient existence with a deeper awareness, whether it be consciousness-raising, revisioning our own religious viewpoints, or just getting on with being in the world in which we live.

But, most of all, you should enjoy Ric Masten's poetry for itself. His latest work is as full of emotions, ideas, and fun as his earlier works. We are sold by this profiting prophet's humor and hope, all the way from TEENAGE CREATURE to this moment, EVEN AS WE SPEAK. Ric Masten has learned not to discard the earlier poetic pages of his life for the later ones. As a poet, his poetry will outlive the "burnout" syndrome and the "planned obsolescence" of a throw-away society. We cannot throw away the experiences of our lives.

If you have finished my "forword," then you have experienced my voice speaking to you, urging you to find your voice, speaking back to Ric Masten's poetry. But even as we speak . . . there are weeds to clear, sunflowers to see, seeds to plant, and songs to sing.

Harvey Solganick
Eastfield College
Dallas Community Colleges
Mesquite, Texas
1982

Even
As We Speak

the future rises
like a swollen stream
the highway sinking in the flood
a pale arm up to its elbow
in a bad dream

like a mad dog
the rushing water tears at our sleeves
we need another crossing
like the one
that hung between two thieves

another skyway
whose boney framework
reaches in both directions
like a poem
able to bear the weight of this parade

and already
voices come from everywhere
gathering in the electric air
even as we speak
a connection is being made

(1982)

1.

Weeds

WEEDS

at 37 general george custer
was still a young man
too full of the media hype
to realize his eden was destined
to be overrun

not that there's anything new
about weeds
and the need to control them

what's new
is being over fifty discovering
that desire gives way to exhaustion
that the nation's leading ground gainer
can suddenly find himself
put on the defense — digging in

   the pig-weed and mustard
   on the war-path again
   along the fence — behind every stone
   cocklebur and crabgrass crouch
   sneaking their tendrils in

not that there's anything new
about another attack of red sorrel

what's new
is this growing sense of battle fatigue
this having to hoe and keep hoeing
knowing how the story
of the little bighorn ends

what's new
is how old it can get
trying to blow the bugle
when you're running low on wind

BAD TASTE

hanging above
her purple naughahyde couch
was the bullfighter
painted on black velvet

> don't you just love
> the way it seems to glow?

she said
and then went on to say
that she considered me
to be
one of the finest poets
writing in america today

J.D. SALINGER GOES INTO THE GARDEN
AND CLOSES THE GATE
or
DRY PERIOD #2

i can think of a verse or two
that slipped through
and turned out to be so stunning
even i
their creator
wonder where they came from

i claim them
but in the same hesitant way
average parents
take credit for a genius child

     they come through us
     they bear our name
     but ?

and what of the newcomers?
the infants
due to be born today
having to do it in the shadow
of those earlier miracles

good poems can be like that
like favored offspring
jealously guarding their place at the table
discouraging the late arrival
by simply being there

my wastebasket fills
with half-formed thoughts
withered ideas
babies
that can never live up

THE POET EXPERIENCES
A PERIOD OF WELL-BEING
or
DRY PERIOD #1

yesterday
feeling no pain
i came that close
to calling up the crisis center

getting on the hot line
to desperately explain
that as an author
i have raked a lot of glowing coals
out of my anxiety and despair
but that recently
things have been going so decently
the fire died
and i haven't even been able
to write an interesting letter

nothing comes

and when a serious writer finds himself
smothered in a state of well-being
the resulting wave of anxiety and despair
makes a call to the crisis center
quite unnecessary

and seized by a fit of depression
i wrote
   if i die
   in an extended dry period
   dig a hole
   and bury me where i lie
   but carry my head out
   bring it back boys
   my mouth
   is loaded with gold

A HOUSEHOLD WORD

orson
it may be a fine wine
but i'm old enough to remember
citizen kane — harry lime
and a time when you were more important
to joseph cotton
than a remedy for headache pain
and don't tell me the dream
wasn't once larger than a cup of coffee
mrs. olsen

i wonder if actors know it's over
when they see themselves
using the right detergent
or is the brainwashing complete
for their sake i hope it is

and what might an over-the-hill poet
be called upon to endorse
not much i would guess
and you can bet
that whatever it might be
wouldn't sell
           alka-selzer
           peanut butter
           drain-o
in the end we're all dead anyway
so what the hell

the day you catch me making commercials
acting the way they do on a TV ad
holding up the truth
looking you straight in the eye
           it's okay
           to feel a little sad

ANOTHER MOTHER POEM

there have been two creatures
on this earth
i could never get the best of
my dog
and my mother

whenever i would catch
either one of them
up to no good
   chewing a shoe
   sneaking through a drawer
one would become deathly ill
the other
pee on the floor

the dog is gone now
piddling around out there
beyond my kick and frustrated shout
and feeling a sudden chill today
i pulled on a sweater
and at the sleeve
guess whose hand came out
   shaking a thermometer

RELATIVITY

have you noticed
that everyone else's kid
seems able
to understand einstein's
theory of relativity?

while yours
can't seem to find the door

we laugh now

but not long ago
a father's misgivings
were kept locked away
on the third floor
like
idiot children

MISSING PERSON REPORT

i distinctly heard you say
you'd be home by ten
and here it is way past one

      late again — the traffic no doubt
      a breakdown — no — a blowout — flares
      in the night — at the hairpin turn
      and the hee-haw hee-haw
      of an ambulance running the lights

      me
      in a ratty old bathrobe
      receiving the call from the highway patrol
      unshaven — disheveled — at the morgue
      grieving out loud as they pull the drawer
      and lift the shroud

      me
      putting aside the hurt
      putting aside the pain
      putting together
      a meaningful memorial service
      down to the last detail
      to the brave smile — the gray rain
      the dirt pile nicely covered by astro turf

      me
      choosing the priest
      the prayer
      the closing song and then

you
come waltzing along
as if nothing had happened
as if nothing were wrong

in the unexpected absence of a loved one
why is a head-on collision easier to imagine

than the thought of them out there
winning the irish sweepstakes?

instead of six feet under the sod
why can't we picture them off somewhere
having the time of their lives
with a rich philanthropist
a theatrical agent
or god?

CHILD PRODIGY

when he was one year old
he was already considered
a world class player
at tic-tac-toe

in his second season
he became a noted semanticist
pointing out to his elders that "maybe"
was just a slow "no"

he was deeply into moby dick
at three
beginning every conversation with:
"call me ishmael"

at four
a recognized poet himself
"till i discovered they were crickets
i had thought they were the stars"

but i knew he was more than bright
when going against popular opinion
he forgave his father for all those
painful trips out to the woodshed

"i had to be whipped"
he said
"you can't send a kid to his room
when the kid has a circus in his head"

RETARDED

TODD (1953-1982)

i still have the pen
you assembled
and what's left of a premonition
that knew

you were too trusting to survive
in the streets of america
too good
like a lamb

among lions
your childish nature was destined
to be misunderstood
to be left

sprawled in the crosswalk
pierced and bleeding
eyes glazing
gazing up through the pain

watching the light turn red
and i
flying to dallas/ft. worth
the day before good friday

see the shadow
of the plane on the earth
and wonder why
in god's name

i should expect
this murdered innocent
to forgive us
for what we did

and didn't do

BACK TO BASICS

from a system of education
wherein if it can't be measured
it will have to be ignored
comes word
> that an entire
> high school assembly
> required to sit through
> a poetry reading
> left at the bell
> convinced
> that they had just had
> a free period

the report
cannot be verified though
as the teaching staff
also took the event
to be a free period
and spent it in limbo
> otherwise known
> as the faculty room

and who can blame them?
they know you only emerge
from something like a spelling bee
with a clear unmistakable winner

the rest of us
the functionally illiterate 5,000
are left
with seven loaves and two fish
to divy up for dinner

> and don't ask for more
> the age of miracles
> is past

A VANISHING SPECIES

i was born on a planet
over fifty light-years from here

an idyllic world
where children grew up
without the threat of nuclear holocaust
or ecological strangulation
no instant systems of communication
no black revolutions
    gay revolutions
    drug revolutions
no women's liberation
not even the choice
of taking or not taking the pill
an eden really

true
the seed of all this was there
but had nothing to do
with my early years

and now
i find myself come to this harsh place
a kind of space traveler
having close encounters with my own children

like creatures
from different star systems
we stare at each other
across the void
even our words have different stems

we are aliens in each other's midst

but damn it
i am the one saddled with the memory
of that other place
part of a colony

stranded on the planet earth
toward the end of the twentieth century
    marooned
      with no way to go back
      and no time to go on

like a moon being eclipsed
my kind will soon be gone
and in light
of where we are today
    the sooner the better

CAR THEFT AND THE BEST POLICY

muhammed said
trust in god but tie your camel

and parking parallel with this
a few simple things you can do to protect
your means of transportation
from the hot-wire artist

— let the paint job oxidize

— always park under a starling

— burn holes in the upholstery

— carpet the dashboard with dead bugs

— spray one fender battleship gray

— replace the antenna with a coat hanger

— store the spare tire in the back seat

— hang the license plate on one screw

— start a beer-can collection on the floor

— save all fast-food debris

do this and you will see
that the life of a car-slob
is worry free

if
however
you choose to drive a status symbol
and flaunt it in the street
and then suffer a vehicular rape
would it be unfair to imply
would i dare imply
that you were asking for it?

ON THE STUMP

anyone
who would want the job
who would allow themselves and their family
to go through
what they know they must go through
to get the job
                  is clearly
someone
we should never let anywhere
near the job

UNCLE TOM

he was a paying customer
as i was
but the way he rushed up to me
with the cream and sugar
you would have thought he worked there

    hey boss
    you'll have to admit
    the service in this place is great!

but i saw the knowing smile
that cracked his black face
and though
i don't usually take anything
with my coffee
this time i did

the soul sister
standing in line behind me
was not amused
everything the old man tried to bring her
she angrily refused

    man
    i don't want to get used to
    something that can't always be

but then
she was too young to know
you can get away with almost anything
if you leave 'em
with a wink at the door

THE CHICKEN OR THE EGG

does life begin
at the moment of conception
or on the birth day?

a rather narrow self-centered quarrel
i would say
a not very great debate

oh — i suppose
when it comes to me
and my starting point
phyllis schlafly is probably right
but the power company did not begin
when they screwed
jerry falwell's light-bulb in

and i seriously doubt
that i would miss myself
if i had never been

at conception
or when the child arrives
in either case
        at either place
life does not begin
it continues
for another generation life survives

THE JUDEO-CHRISTIAN
CHAIN-SAW MASSACRE

in crowded commons such as these
you with your chain-saw
missionary attitude
should really give some thought
to how it would be
if you did succeed in clearing away
the volunteers
that spring up around the monument

revealing the truth
is a labor of love i'm sure
but given only one place to roost
can you imagine
what a flock of pigeons this size
would do
to a single piece of statuary?

i say
let the truth
stay hidden in the woods
surrounded by a variety of trees
with branches enough
to give all the cuckoos
a place to perch
                    or better still
put it in poetry
where a thing can be true
even though it didn't happen

and no
apologies needed

CLUTCHING AT STRAWS

she said
that he said
he was seeing other women
and loving it

she said
the words hurt
but that she took solace
in the plural

knowing
what i know
there was enough pathos
in that statement

to almost be
a poem

A DRINKING PROBLEM

RSVP — and we do respond don't we?
gussying up for the grand event
          the stepsisters
          dressing and undressing
          the prince breathing into his hand
          testing his breath
          rapunzel with her fine tooth comb
insecurity
working like a worm in a winesap

all that time and attention
all that fuss and bother
that mirror mirror on the wall business
all that
just to get past self-doubt
and on to the gala affair
where above the noise and din
someone can shout

          come on in
          and name your poison

— and we do respond don't we?

the worm turning here
to quickly demolish the image
that had seemed so important in the glass
on the outside of the door
the spit and polish dissolving
in the glass on the inside 'til:
          cinderella is out of her shoes
          the heir to the throne
          puking on the floor
          and coming undone before our eyes
          rapunzel
          really letting her hair down

and don't think you can avoid

the transformation
by avoiding the drink
in situations such as these
a non-drinker has a drinking problem too

my abstinence
making me appear like a grumpy giant
a bad-tempered troll
my sobriety
taken as a clear reflection on present company

> and when snow white is into the apples
> she wants nothing to do with a mirror

AN IDENTITY CRISIS

i know an actor
who had the lead in a major soap
for seven years he played the part
of ted
      or brad
            or bart
i could never remember
but for seven years that was who
he was
         one morning he reported to work
and was informed
that he was about to be killed
in an unexpected car wreck
just like that
         after which
he was told to pick up his check

since then
he hasn't been able to find work
even though the folks in K-Mart
still come up and say
            hi bart
       or brad
     or ted
i could never remember
              imagine
spending the rest of your life
trying to learn how to live
with being dead

or is this just an extreme example
of what
we are all trying to do

THE AGING PROCESS

the aging process proceeds
the latest wrinkle
being
that i can't go to the movies
the theater
or anywhere else these days
without first
taking a little afternoon nap

without one
i am in grave danger
of paying hard-earned money
to spend an evening sleeping upright
in a room full of strangers

THE BALD POEM

getting a little thin on top
aren't you sport?

my neanderthal brothers
get a kick
out of razzing me this way

and i am going bald
but what would you have me do?
nurture and cultivate a sideburn
till it hangs down like a house plant
like a long trailing fern
to rake across my barren crown

or would you prefer a transplant?
my naked pate a parade ground
where rows of foreign follicles
stand stiffly
like the michigan state marching band
poised to play the national anthem

perhaps a toupee? a saucy little pompadour
that when not in use
lies around the house like a lapdog
like the dusty pelt of a pekingese
which i suspect smells of musty tapestry

do this to my head?
no way — not me
like the granite dome
that presides over yosemite valley
i would not be what i am
with trees

my scalp is bare
but gentlemen
look at it this way

we all begin with roughly
the same number of hormones

and if you want to blow yours
growing hair ...

A CAPTIVE AUDIENCE

anamosa
lay in the gray midwestern afternoon
like a whale in shallow water

inside
jonah counted time on the ribs
with a tin cup

and no one was sure
a poetry reading
in a penitentiary
wouldn't be considered
cruel and unusual punishment

the question however
was eloquently answered
when the warden had the speaker
forcibly removed from the stage

    get the poet out of here
    he raged
    can't you see
    the prisoners are escaping

THE PRISON ROUTINE

i wish i could say i was tired
of the prison routine
of rising each day
to find the work laid out before me
of being told where to go
and what to do

always laboring on someone else's dream

but lately i have found
that a dream realized is a dream lost
and that the boss
also cries himself to sleep at night
feeling caught in a web
not of his own making

it would seem then
that freedom and self-determination
do not lie in the act
of choosing the place where i will be
but rather
that i be in the place where
i am

and as of now at least
the spider
is nowhere in sight

FOR A SON-IN-LAW
A MEMO FROM THE PAST

at 25
you can't imagine how frustrating it is
to be over 50
trying to explain something
to someone 25

to someone — who is twice as far away
                from tomorrow
                as I am

to someone — on whose person
                things have not begun growing
                and /or
                started dropping off
                and falling out of

to someone — who hasn't yet discovered
                that being old
                feels exactly like being young
                with something wrong

and so
for those of you who maintain
chronological age is irrelevant
i have prepared a statement
to be opened and read when
they themselves turn fifty
a memo that goes:

                greetings
                know-it-all
                and don't say i didn't tell ya so.

(the anticipation of an event such as this
is incentive enough to keep me alive
for another 25 years)

trolling
the california mental-health scene
with a two day seminar: Depression Syndrome —
An Astrological Vegetarian Holistic Approach

the catch
was for the most part
native to the pacific coast
flounders — groupers
left in the wake of Prop. 13
what you might expect
except
for two migrating easterners

    a deep water psychiatrist
    who took copious notes in a perfect hand
    his eyes had a bugged look
    but under pressure his gaze never wavered
and
    a female child psychologist
    a spiney thing in a tailored tweed suit
    who retreated into a hard-cover book
    whenever approached

even before orientation was over
they had found each other
and like sharks
formed a silent alliance
a disturbing presence
that had the rest of us running like grunion
darting around
intellectualizing
unable to risk and grow
knowing there was something alien
in the water

    sizing us up
    rolling its eyes

exchanging looks that ranged from pain
to pity

a couple of cold fish
in the house of aquarius

     ***

next day however
the sea-world analogy
began to come apart

     for the psychologist
it happened at coffee break
when mildly amused by something
she smiled
and in that brief softening
i could see that she was quite pretty

     the psychiatrist?
he kept that pencil going
until just before noon
when he startled us all
with a robert-penn-warren-type poem
about wanting to grow up
and be like his youngest son

after lunch they didn't return
somewhat relieved
and at the same time disappointed
the rest of us came together
for a warm california closing
om

     what happened to them?
only they know
perhaps they went on
to spend the afternoon together
in san francisco

     two lonely people
three thousand miles from the ocean
living out
the kind of sophisticated story
you only find in the new yorker

SYBIL'S SONG

when sybil comes
she comes with doors and windows
and you can see your mountain
through her eyes
when sybil comes
she draws aside the curtains
and the lilac and the lupine
take you by surprise

    your vision has been clouded
    your eyes no longer see
    then sybil comes
    and as she looks around
    you will find the ocean
    right where it used to be
    with tiny freighters
    steaming up and down

when sybil comes
the cobwebs turn to flowers
and you will see your gardens
are in bloom
when sybil comes
we'll have children in the morning
gypsies in the canyons
all the afternoon

    then out on the veranda
    we sip our burgundy
    and sit and watch
    the sun begin to fall
    you've seen a million sunsets
    but each time sybil comes
    you realize
    you haven't seen them all

when sybil comes
she also brings a parting
and something would be lost
if she should stay
and so it goes
the sunlight and the shadow
the coming and the going
and today

11.

Sunflowers

SUNFLOWERS

no
even if i could have
i would not have
spared van gogh
the pain of cutting
his ear off
and robbed myself
of those
sunflowers

sorry about that vincent
sorry about that
myself

(1970)

PING PONG

sometimes i leave the door ajar
just a crack
and the people in the market place
pause for thirty seconds
peeking through
looking at the meat on the counter
seeing if it is fit for human consumption

most of them pass on
they have their reasons
but once in a while someone slips in
to catch the show
sometimes they come up afterwards
and speak to my songs
so i do an encore

which isn't very existential of me
especially when i don't know
what i'm going to be when i grow up
perhaps we should play ping pong
if the ball keeps coming back across the net
at least we both know somebody's there
and that's what it's all about anyway

THE COFFEE TABLE DANCER

i remember parties
when i was only five
standing at the window
watching the guests arrive
they'd step into the hallway
laughing too loud i'd think
keeping their fingers busy
with a cigarette and a drink
and i'd be in the corner
in a white shirt and short pants
standing in the corner
just waiting for my chance
      the coffee table dancer
      oh just you wait and see

they'd sit down together
to play at their head games
to quote the books they were reading
and drop the authors' names
the talk was always liberal
around the onion dip
but lonely were the faces
with the talking lips
and i'd be in the corner
and not receive a glance
standing in the corner
just waiting for my chance
      the coffee table dancer
      oh just you wait and see

they'd interrupt each other
fighting for the floor
to mourn the league of nations
and weep about the war
and when their lips were finished
with what was in their head
they'd fall strangely silent
for it had all been said

and then i'd leave the corner
for this would be my chance
to jump up on the table
and do my little dance
        the coffee table dancer
        see me — see me — see me

and now here i am before you
and i think i'm living a lie
what devious means i'm using
just to catch your eye
and was i not more honest
when i was young and green
coffee table dancing
just so i'd be seen?
hey — you there in the corner
won't you take this chance
to jump up on the table
and join me in a dance
        coffee table dancers
        aren't we all
        aren't we all
        aren't we all?

A PERFECT RED STRIPE

years ago it was there
your beauty
on something as simple as a square of paper

remember kindergarten?
and the yellow spot — the sun
    the splash of blue — the sky
    the curving
    dripping green line of the hills
and the perfect red stripe

remember how you looked at your work
and saw that it was good?

    what is this?
    teacher said

    a fire engine
and then you looked at your work again
and then you hurled your brush
into the corner of the room
and stomped off defeated

later
out on the playground
you hit barbara jenkins in the head
with a kickball
and now you sit in the barber chair
hating yourself and the length of my hair
waiting for some kind of good fairy
to come down and save your ass

    but i remember
    i wish you did

KINDERGARTEN LOGIC

how many mornings have i struggled
on the forest floor
trying to pull my pants on
inside a sleeping bag

cursing and muttering
in the darkness of that collapsible hole
looking for all the world
like some stricken giant green bug
writhing on the ground in its death throes

this morning i awoke clearheaded
and decided to stand like a man
and do it the easy way
and i did
and was stepping into them
just as slick as you please

when i heard this voice whispering

    someone will see you!

and in the chilly morning air
of that crowded campground
i stood there
pants half-mast
and thought about that
and it came to me in a blinding flash
the reason
we don't offer a course in logic
to kindergarten kids

SPIDERS!

when i was a little kid
another little kid told me
that if i poured water down a tarantula hole
i could get him to come out
so i did
      and he did
and bit me

since then spiders
have not been among my favorite things

last year i had occasion
to spend some time with an entomologist
that's a bug freak
and this nut was really into spiders
      beautiful creatures
that walk smoothly
four feet on the floor
not jerky like people
this dude didn't live in a house
he lived in a big jar full of 'em

and i got to thinking
that if someone ran up to us in the street
yelling
      spiders!
we'd 'a' both known
what he was hollering about
but we would 'a' knocked each other down
running in different directions

      when it comes to words
      it's a miracle we communicate at all

ELLEN AND I

my youngest daughter
likes to ride
to the mailbox with me

she fetches the mail
while i turn the car around
then she climbs into the back seat

and doles out my letters
slowly
inspecting each envelope

till i am infuriated
and turn red
and shout at her

ellen!
gimme
the letters!

my youngest daughter likes to do this
it is one of the few times
she has my full attention

***

and i have had this beard of mine
for twenty-four years now
for twenty-four years

my chin
has been kept well under cover
and the best thing i can tell you about it

is how
it still bugs the hell
out of my mother

THE WEANING

after considerable work in the field
i have come to the conclusion
that when it comes to me
and my children
it is easy to say "no" all the time
and it is easy to say "yes" all the time
but it is impossible
to be a logical consistent parent

however
i do not lie awake nights
over this any longer
for to treat children
in a logical consistent fashion
and then turn them out into the world
as we know it
would be a cruel crippling inhuman thing to do

it is only fair though
that when the kids have broken loose
and are out on their own
they should receive a hand-written letter
from me their father
expressing my love
and stating that all is forgiven
if they promise not to come home

(1970)

CLARITY

on the marquee — THE REVOLUTION
now playing

and clarity sits in her crystal room
watching us pass
dispensing tickets and information
through a hole in the glass

   does it have a happy ending?
i inquired

and her small clear voice
was a wind chime in my ear

   do you really think for a moment
   hitler in his bunker
   his back to the wall
   would not have taken us all with him
   if he'd had a button to push?

do you really think for a moment
the brass in the pentagon
the kremlin
peking
does not contain the same basic elements?

you pulled your eye-teeth at hiroshima

hey dinosaur
did you ever wish that you were small?

THE MILLENNIUM

he had $13.67 in his pocket
when they busted him
for stealing a package of gum
from the supermarket
and what is this all about?

we turn right at third street
and there it is
a mormon artist's conception
of the millennium
the flags are up

waving us
into a glittering asphalt marina
it is a time of celebration
it is always may day
on the shopping mall

we are drawn across sweeping lawns
past dancing fountains
into majestic buildings
to wheel bright shining baskets
down festive aisles

piled high with old friends
whose names once learned
are unforgettable
each package psychologically
designed to seduce us

the merchants
are becoming behavioral scientists
and a practicing christian
i know
has become a thief

THE LIGHT BRINGERS

as a child
i remember my father
taking me to the beach
on dark nights
to see the phosphorus
        the light bringers
tiny organisms
i don't know their official
scientific name
but at certain times of the year
they would come
        billions of them
washing into our coastal waters
and we would go
and walk the waterline
like gods
making firey footprints
        in the sand

        they light up as they die
        father would say
        and i would stamp my foot
        delighted

perhaps we too have crawled
from that very same sea
and evoluted to the place
where we will burn ourselves
from the heavens
        in nuclear holocaust

and watching from afar
two mantis-like creatures
standing on a grassy hillock
will touch anterior legs
as we flame out
        whispering excitedly

                shooting star
                make a wish

I AM

one of these days
in a clean white smock
we will pull a switch
and lock in empathy
there will follow a spin
                a click
and then a computer
will drop a card that says
simply: I AM
                on that day
cold applause
will rattle in the laboratory
the first machine
has found itself

the happy scientist
can now retire to light his pipe
and turn to the evening times
where he will find
that while he was busy
with his program
he poisoned the water and air
past the point of repair
in twenty years
only the clockwork
will remain
                but then
stepping back
and surveying the scene
have we — humankind
not done all
that we were meant to do
being but one small link
in the evolution of the machine?

carry it on IBM

50

THE WILDERNESS

three days
lost in the wilderness
all alone
and i can't describe the ecstasy
of discovering
that discarded six-pack of beer cans

       found!
       i'm found!

like dogs lifting our legs
making things more familiar
we hurry around the countryside
urinating aluminum and plastic containers

taking color slides from speeding windows
so that later in the safety of suburbia
we can project the image
of where we've been
onto our own wrinkled sheets

but go up on the back of a mountain
and explain that little man
you with a history
of killing what you can't understand

could it be
that there is more to it
than the greed of our strip mine
and the thoughtless trail
of our broken bottles?

could it be
we are murdering the earth
to be done with the uncomfortable question
of our own existence?

       could it be?

HUMMINGBIRD

working in the garden
bent over the dark earth
i the man with the hoe
lost in the planting
when sound has called my eyes up
and there
hanging just above me — a hummingbird
christ-like
the two of us frozen in the spell
of this suspended moment

     hummingbird — hummingbird
     hanging in the air
     fills me with wonder
     just seeing you there

then darting off
seeming to fall over a rim of green
he's gone and i after him
through a glass door
jingling
entering pet store noise
where amid mynah-bird curses
and monkey screams
the pekingese lady sells me the 26th verse
chapter one — genesis

     hummingbird — hummingbird
     magic are your wings
     but we have dominion
     over all living things

a perky pet hummingbird feeder
$1.49 — the cheap ones are best
i'm told
fill glass blossom with water
dropping in
one hummingbird-feeder food tab

shaking well and hanging same
just outside kitchen window
then i — sky fisherman — sit down to wait

> hummingbird — hummingbird
> here is something sweet
> bring me your magic
> and i'll give you a treat

and he comes — hovering — cautious
like a street-wise child
until inches from my eyes
he threads pink sugardrop with needle beak
backs off — comes again — and again
hooked now
by this inexhaustible scarlet crystal flower
returning so often
finally he bores me till the act
of filling the feeder becomes work

> hummingbird — hummingbird
> i tire of your tricks
> you've become a junky bird
> coming for your fix

now no longer busy
visiting the sweet fountains of the field
all alone like america he sits on a twig
fat — guarding the great glass goodie
his bronze head — a helmet
blinding — flashing — angry red
vicious — he attacks all intruders
and god is in the kitchen
and all's well with the world

> hummingbird — hummingbird
> what have we done
> why does the mountain
> swallow the sun

MY BARN

i pause in the road
and look back to my barn
a shed really
but it is mine
and i say it's a barn

i can see where the new nails
shine in the braille of weathered wood
well-wintered wood
snatched from the path
of a mindless caterpillar

i played the priest and preacher
with those unhappy planks
and salvaged every stick i could
and stood them up again
to be my barn

but now — pausing in the road
i am uneasy
my apron is heavy with these idle nails
and yet back there my barn is built
and i have all this time to kill

CHRISTMAS CARDS
IN THE MIDDLE OF JULY

in a telephone booth
opening my christmas cards
in the middle of july
and on the telephone
sweet billie was asking me
if i wouldn't like to come
and drop by
        i said
tell me how to get there
        she said
tell me where you are
        so i told her
i'm in a telephone booth
opening my christmas cards
in the middle of july

she said: take a look around
can you see a sign?
i said: no i'm blind in my good eye
but i think i'm busted down
somewhere on the road
between my birth
and where i'm gonna die
        so just
tell me how to get there
        she said
tell me where you are
        i said i told you
i'm in a telephone booth
opening my christmas cards
in the middle of july

she said: i'm getting awful tired of you
not making any sense
and she started in to cry
and when i tried to apologize
billie started saying things

gonna wind up
in a "good-by"
             i said
tell me how to get there
             she said
well tell me where you are
             i said
if i knew that would i be
             in a telephone booth
             opening my christmas cards
             in the middle of july

so just
tell me how to get there
she said: tell me where you are
i said: i don't know that
             so just tell me how to get there
she said
     good-by
         hung up
             left me
in a telephone booth
opening my christmas cards
in the middle of july

MARVIN

marvin was lickin' the walls
when we entered
i think his mother drove him to it
the way she hovered around
like the reality
on the other side of the door there

now don't act crazy marvin dear
just sing us a song

and he did
turning like a child with his arms out
trying to get dizzy
but you could hear him if you listened
hear him clear
so i answered with a song of my own
about a caterpillar

and when i looked up
i found him sane as i am
crazy just like me
and we laughed and talked together like this
for more than an hour

or at least until his mother returned
to give him a hand-painted tie
which was just what he needed
he said "good-by" then — with his eyes
and went back to lickin' the walls

i guess freedom
freedom
is simply being able to choose
your own kind of cage

ain't that right marvin?

COMMUNICATION

communication is my thing
and i'll gladly show you
how my knuckles bleed
as i go from door to door — knocking
and it pleases me to tell you
how i've wept into an open phone

is anybody home?
is anybody home?
communication is my thing

but once
while running my prepared speech
i paused for effect and heard breathing
you were there
i mean really there
and i became afraid

so hanging up
i went outside and looked around
until i found three deadly stones
and then i set off with my trusty sling

communication — that's my thing

FLAGS

she dresses in flags
and comes on
like a mack truck
she paints
her eyelids green
and her mouth
is a loudspeaker
rasping out profanity

at cocktail parties
she is everywhere
like a sheep dog
working a flock
nipping at your sleeve
spilling your drink
bestowing
wet sloppy kisses

but i
have received
secret messages
carefully written
from the shy
quiet woman
who hides
in this bizarre
gaudy castle

HONESTY

third period recess
was the battleground of my childhood
and i
was such a skinny little squirt
why any one of those big kids
with the big teeth
could have walked off with all my marbles
anytime he wanted

but i learned
how to whip 'em with my mouth
when one of them would grab me
by the shirt front
and describe
how he was gonna demolish me
i would smile like a medieval saint
softly saying
and you're just the bully to do it

hell
i always had more marbles
than i knew what to do with

look out for honesty
it can be a form of brutality
look out for the weeping ones
who unload first in an encounter group
they'll be back to get you later

     but i told you i was a plastic phony
     a chauvinist pig
     that talks too much
     i told you that honesty
     can be a form of brutality

if i can tell you before you can tell me
i'm home safe

i only hope i have the peace of mind

on my death bed
to look up into the face
of death descending
remembering to say

   and you're just the bully to do it!

WHEN IT'S ALL BEEN SAID

well that's it
i have nothing more to say
i said
and went on to play many variations
on this theme

i said it upstairs
          downstairs
          in the kitchen
          in the bedroom
nothing more to say
it's finished

i'm going to bed
where i will set the electric blanket
at body temperature
take the fetal position
and wait it out

i put the dust cover on my quiet
typewriter
and laid it to rest beside my deceased
grandmother

i mean what can you say
when it's all been said
and like a pat on the head
you smile
          perhaps we could try silence
          for awhile

AS I FLEW BY

i'm still thinking about you
hitchhiker
you who i passed yesterday
who gave me such a sunny smile
and moved your thumb
with such grace
and style

my old car
my homesick snail
is the kind that you depend on
i know that
and you looked so surprised
and hurt
as i flew by

i watched you watching me
out of sight
in the rear view mirror
we both lost something friend
i know that
but there was no time
to stop and tell you

that
i was rushing to my funeral

A BENT CANARY

i looked down at her
perched in that chromium bird cage
hands resting on the thin rubber tires
legs stacked in front of her
a bent canary
but singing brightly

> you don't know what happiness is
> she sang
> until you see a paraplegic
> rolling off to his first day of work

the height of my high
is directly proportionate
to the depth of my low
and then lightly
over her shoulder
wheeling away

> lucky
> lucky me

and she meant it
she really meant it

A WEEK BEFORE THE WRECK

nathan is
but nathan doesn't know it yet

so he comes in a cloud of dust
and he has removed the muffler
from his machine
and we can hear him coming
for ten minutes
hair wild
shirt open
a scar on his hard young belly
he steals my wine
rolls cigarettes
and he can spit at least fifteen feet
nathan can

and even before his dust has settled
he is gone
with my boy down the road
shouting and yelling

nathan
i hope you look down soon
and find your shadow
before you hurt yourself
and/or all of us

FOR JOSH

the three of them came in
the three women
sobbing
for the young man
who had stood awkwardly
in this very room
only yesterday
come to see my daughters
with his friends
like young playful dogs

i must remember him quickly
while i still can
blond hair — about my size
with blue eyes
i'm not sure of this though
i say blue because mine are blue
and he reminded me of myself
long ago

my wife weeps for our son
who is off on a camping trip
and for the other mother
who becomes herself
and of course the boy

   do you think he knew we liked him?

my daughters weep
for all the tomorrows
that can never be
the kisses — laughter and promises
broken on the rocks
and maybe because the sense
escapes them
and they must turn to mythology
which is also
something to weep about

and i am sick inside
and sad
because i already grow tired of this
and by evening
i will have forgotten

THE TRAIN

he must have made up his mind in the night
because after a cheerful breakfast
he quietly left the house
walked to the railroad yard
where he sat down and waited
his cheek resting on the cold steel rail
three hours he waited for
the train to come and it came
                              three hours

that's a long time — a lifetime
what did he do with it?
did he wander back through the weed patch
of his nineteen years
enjoying what few flowers had bloomed there
or did he wait like so many of us
with nothing more on his mind
                              than
the train is coming
the train is coming
the train is co—
                 father of the boy
and mother
i am here and at the same time with you
and i am crying for chris
who caught the acid train out of here
and for you
and that's all right
for how else would i know what laughter was?

at times
one looks back on his accomplishments
and they do seem meaningless
and i have looked at the books and records
i have produced for sale
those spiritual experiences you can purchase
and relive in the privacy of your living room
as just so much bullshit

.   and then your letter
describing the dark dark night you spent
all alone with my words
the note ending with your simple thanks
and i am reminded of a wise old man
who once rapped me with his cane
and said
            do not say bullshit to be profane
            it is used to help things
            live and grow

DRAGONFLY LOST

i was really born when i was 13 years old
standing beside my father's pale stiff body
in that screaming crashing moment
i completely forgot how to be
a dragonfly
but painful as it is at times
i gladly pay the price
to be aware of my own little 4th of july

> the dragonfly is not very lonely
> that's true
> but he doesn't know where his handle is
> either

and i must tell you "i love you" now
while i still have the chance
i never told my father
never bothered to yell through an open moment

> hey dad
> i love you

there would always be time for that later
right? and anyhow i was too busy doing
my little dragonfly thing over the pool

> the dragonfly is not very lonely
> that's true
> but he has no ticket to the now
> either

yes i love you
you commie faggot punk — you establishment pig
you honky devil — you nigger
you dirty old man — you smart-assed kid
for haven't we all stood helplessly
in hospital halls and put children on buses
and haven't we all been to the grave
together

the dragonfly is not very lonely
that's true
but he has found no common ground
either

and the dragonfly does not know what
together is for he has never been apart
he sleeps in the garden ignoring the apple
but think about it people — think about it
would you give up the happiest day of your life
in fair exchange
to be rid of the most hopeless — lonely
and despairing one?
i doubt it

no
the dragonfly is not very lonely
pity the poor dragonfly

HALF THE TIME

when i am joyous
and i am half the time
joyous is what i am
and i refuse to drive these moments off
composing poetry about them

i'm having a good time at the party
ta da-da da da-da ta dee

if i do this
i will soon rhyme myself
right back into misery
and wreck the party

but when i feel hopeless
lonely and despairing
when i think about death
i begin to discover where i am

feeling myself

so i will continue
to worry the canker sore on my soul
in order to be more fully
present
and accounted for

THE MORNINGS

i'd be in good shape
if it wasn't for the dark empty hole
i wake up to every morning

the tiger pit
with the sharp stakes
waiting at the bottom
i balance on the edge feeling scared
lethargic
sick
looking down into the darkness
imagining a thousand pointed tomorrows

sometimes
it takes the better part of a day
to fill it with smooth stones
and get across and out onto the ridge
where one can see the ocean

SING A SONG
(a gospel approach to zen)

in a tiny rowboat
tryin' to cross a river
tryin' to make it to the other shore
a young man and an old man
stuck out in the middle
when a sudden storm swept away the oars

cut off from the safety
of the solid ground they'd come from
too far to get to where they longed to go
the situation was hopeless
helplessly they drifted
to the waterfall that waited just below

like a leaf in a gutter
captured on the water
the ragin' river washing them along
they only had a moment
till they'd be carried over
so they stood up in the boat and sang a song

    sing a song
    sing a song
    when hope has been abandoned
    sing a song
    brother it would be a real catastrophe
    if you should fail to stand and sing a song

crashin' through the jungle
here came this foreign feller
a hungry tiger closin' in behind
chased him to a canyon
the poor man tumbled over
but as he fell he caught a passin' vine

helplessly he dangled
while up above the tiger
settled down to play a waiting game

the vine would never hold him
old it was and rotten
and down below another tiger came

but a berry bush was growin'
there on the bank before him
and it held a single berry ripe and red
he took the tender morsel
and in the final moment
delicious! that is what they say he said

    sing a song
    sing a song
    when hope has been abandoned
    sing a song
    brother it would be a real catastrophe
    if you should fail to stand and sing a song

waterfalls and tigers
somethin's gonna get ya
we're here today tomorrow we'll be gone
it's the sound of one hand clappin'
and if ya try to fight it
brother you're gonna miss the song

111.

Sunflowers Seeds

The protest

The profit motive

THE PROTEST BIZ

Got a call the other day, got a buzz from Sodom
Down near Mickey Mouse land.
Man says: I hear ya got songs Baby? Protest songs 'bout peace
    and labor strikes, freedom songs of civil rights.
And I said: Yes, it's true. An' he says: Cool baby cool!
Says: I think you're a damn fool
But I never let politics stand between me and money.
I'm gonna make us both a bundle, Sweetie!
I think you're a pink fink
But that's the way it is in the protest biz!

Said: I want ya to sign on the dotted line, Sweetie
I want ya to point your finger for me
at thirty-three and a third.
I'll put your picture
All psychedelic and like that on the record jacket,
With your big guitar and your long hair hangin' down.
But I'm goin' bald, I said.
And he said: Oh, I'm sorry, I must have the wrong number.
But I got a beard, says I. Groovy! says he,
I think you're a damn red an' I wish you were dead
But like I said:
That's the way it is in the protest biz.

Are you interested? I said: No, I don't think so.
He said: Now don't blow your cool, Sweetheart!
Watcha writin' them songs for?
Ya want to reach the people, don'tcha?
Well, come to me, Baby, if ya got a message,
Not Western Union.
Who do you think you're reachin'
singin' to the walls like that?
Come to me, Baby, if ya want to be heard.
I'll make ya rich and famous
Ya dirty Commie!
But that's the way it is in the protest biz.

Well I think it's a lousy way to make a buck, I said.
Now, don't point your finger at me, Babe!
Like where would you be without war and Watts
And poverty. Without labor strikes and tragedy,
You'd be out of business, Sweetie,
with nothin' to sing about!
Beautiful, I said,
I'll sing about faith, hope and charity.
It won't sell, Man! he said.
And I said: Mister ...
And he said: Call me Sweetheart!
So I said: Sweetheart. An' he said: Yeah?
And I said: Go to hell!
And he said: Well, that's the way it is in the protest biz.
And then he hung up.

(1967)

TALK ABOUT

i don't wanna talk about peace
my babies are cryin' for bread
how can we reason together ol' friend
'til all my family is fed
and i don't wanna talk about
world brotherhood
and everyone actin' so nice
i wanna talk about cuttin' the pie
where i gonna get me a slice
       no — i don't wanna talk about
       don't talk about — talk about peace
       i wanna talk about — let's talk about
       somethin' to eat

you like to talk about love
as you shove the food in your face
i count the ribs of my children ol' friend
and find that they add up to hate
and i don't wanna hear about
the money you sent
it went in the dictator's bank
i wanna hear about breakin' some bread
and not demandin' my thanks
       no — i don't wanna talk about
       don't talk about — talk about peace
       i wanna talk about — let's talk about
       somethin' to eat

i don't wanna talk about peace
and layin' my guns at my feet
i'll keep a-pullin' the trigger ol' friend
till I get me somethin' to eat
you better call out an army
of well-fed police
we're comin' to break down the door
the haves and have nots 'll have at it again
and the name of the game is war
       no — i don't wanna talk about

don't talk about — talk about peace
i wanna talk about — let's talk about
somethin' to eat

no i don't give a damn about peace
i live in the land of have not
as long as the poor are among you ol' friend
your cold wars are gonna get hot
and meat on the table
bread on the plate
it won't solve all our problems ol' friend
but till i get me somethin' tucked under my belt
the talkin' can't even begin
no — i don't wanna talk about
don't talk about — talk about peace
i wanna talk about — let's talk about
somethin' to eat

IN MY OWN FUNNY WAY

i was given four white pigeons
young birds put in my care
and i built them a loft
where they might stay
you can say it was a prison
but i meant it for a home
and i brought them feed and water
every day
                    you see i loved them
                    no matter what you say
                    god knows i loved them
                    in my own funny way

and i promised them their freedom
promised them the sky
but only when i knew
they wouldn't stray
and i warned them of the hunter
who hunted on the hill
and of the hawk who waited
for her prey
                    you see i loved them
                    no matter what you say
                    god knows i loved them
                    in my own funny way

and then there came the morning
i forgot to hook the gate
in an instant they were out
and in a tree
and i worried myself crazy
trying to coax them back
but they paid little mind to me

and i thought about the hunter
and i thought about the hawk
and i saw that they
were bound to fly away

so i went and took my shotgun
down from the wall
and the thunder of it sounded
in the day
          but i loved them
          no matter what you say
          god knows i loved them
          in my own funny way

                      (Kent State)

WORDS ARE WEIRD AND HUMANS ... ?

Sometimes the English language
Will abandon you completely.
Like, have you ever gone looking for the word
You would use to describe
What it was you had left if you happened to lose
One of your galoshes?
What is that other rubber thing?
And goulash is Hungarian stew.

And I've got a "new" for you.
"New" being the singular of "news",
Which is that words are weird,
And the weirdest words of all are the obscenities.
Like who invented these?
Where did they come from?

Did the English-speaking part of the world
Once hold a great convention?
The chair calling the restless throng to order,
Explaining that some ding dong
Would soon invent the automobile.
A thing
That would forever be breaking down,
Running out of gas and catching our fingers
In slamming doors.
                    Aghhhhh!

And for sanity's sake at least,
We should set aside some forbidden words to use
At times such as these,
To help let the steam out.
And rising to the occasion
A man of vision shouts from the back of the hall
"Mr. Chairperson!"
    (I'm for degenderization, but what do we do
    with words like: manhole?) "I suggest
That in the English-speaking part of the world
We use bodily functions as our obscenities."

The motion was seconded.
Carried unanimously.
The jubilant congregation staging
A wild twenty-minute demonstration,
Before settling down to the difficult task
Of hammering out the details,
Taking the most intimate human bodily function
And making it the most obscene.
Then completing the list,
Heavy on body parts and toilet procedure.

Clearly
It was one of humankind's finest hours,
And it simply had to be this way,
Because in other cultures,
What we consider obscene and insulting,
Means no more to them than like calling
A person: A big eye!
A little ear!
The son of a forehead!
In the Orient, however,
Try calling a person: A pig!
Or a dog and see what happens.

I would guess at their great gathering
a dignified old gentleman rose to propose:
That here in the East
To call a human by an animal name
Should be the highest of insults.
And of course,
For this wisdom and insight, he was given
A standing but polite: Ahhh so!

And so it goes until every radio/TV talk show
Keeps a finger on the panic button: (beep beeping)
Out expletives
That have become so commonplace and innocuous,
Even sweet old ladies are overheard at teatime saying

Margaret, would you prefer one or two
(beep beep) lumps?

And why?
Everyone knows what goes on behind the (beep beeps).
It must be that the media realizes
How overworked and useless these words have become,
And is now breaking ground for the day,
That when we stub our toe we can go hopping around
(beep beeping).

Perhaps now is the time
For another great obscenity assembly.
Time to outline this new dilemma
and once again throw the floor open for suggestions
So that
The ever-present man of brilliance
Can propose to thunderous applause:
Mr. Chairperson, the old words have become impotent,
So I suggest we change and make the word:
Nose
The filthiest dirtiest word in the English language.
After which, I suppose we would all
Step into the street going: Nose! Man, nose!
Kiss my nose!
Up your nose!

There is a sad postscript to all of this
However, which is
That in the name of tolerance
And understanding the Free Speech Movement
Has become so successful
We may have lost more than we gained.
For I find
I am left with nothing to use profane enough,
Obscene enough; To describe the stupid waste and tragic death
of Lenny Bruce.

(1965)

DEAR SANTA

the wife and i separated
why, well let's just say because
and today i got the letter
my boy wrote to santa claus
it read ...

    dear santa bring home my daddy
    on this christmas day
    mommy has never quit cryin'
    since daddy went away

    this christmas forget the presents
    i don't want any toys
    santa i just want a daddy
    like other girls and boys

    i guess you know i been naughty
    don't know why i can't be good
    but santa if you bring my daddy
    i promise i'll act like i should

    dear santa on christmas mornin'
    when i run to see the tree
    there with his arm around mommy
    please have daddy waitin' for me

i cried as i read that letter
and i knew, i knew that i had done wrong
so i'm goin' home this christmas
cause home is where i belong

santa, now don't you worry
i'll be beside that tree
and i'll have my arm around mommy
when my boy comes lookin' for me

             (1959)

TEENAGE CREATURE

i was a teenage creature
tonight there's a werewolf moon
come and hold my hairy hand
down at the black lagoon

i was a high school monster
a teenage frankenstein
let me take you in my arms
and crush you one more time

gotta a face like a dog
feet like a frog
i'm covered with a lizard's scale
gotta cut a hole in my ol' blue jeans
for my slimy tail

i was a body snatcher
and you're the sweet earthling
do you think that you would dare
go steady with the thing?

i was a teenage vampire
a rock and rollin' ghoul
won't you let a dracula
walk you home from school?

i live in a hole
look like the mole
a horrible sight to see
if you hear a growl i'm on the prowl
and baby you're for me

i was a teenage spider
and your my junior miss
so give a boy tarantula
his very first kiss

i was a teenage creature
i'm always scaring you
so point a stake straight at my heart
and darling drive it through

(1958)

Philosophers And Poets
by Robert O'Brien

Psychology And A Wizard
by Roberta Richards

*A Teacher Looks At
Ric Masten: One Of Our Failures*
by G. Lynn Nelson

Backwords

PHILOSOPHERS AND POETS

Over the last 20 years, Ric Masten and I have often talked about the differences between philosophers and poets. After Plato initiated the quarrel, philosophers and poets have tended to avoid each other. Poets, I have noticed, seldom ask philosophers to write introductions to their work. We speak a different language. Our estrangement seems to be confirmed by the difference between thinking and feeling, objectivity and subjectivity, abstract and concrete, rational and irrational, literal and figurative. In each of these dichotomies the philosopher stands on one side and the poet on the other. Or so it seems.

Images/Ideas

Ric calls himself a "speaking poet." Like Homer, he is a story teller. He puts ideas into images. In doing so he comes up against Plato's epistemic objections. Plato maintained that philosophy seeks reality through the analysis of ideas, while poetry deals with mere appearances in the form of images. Yet the moment we hear this formula we are dissatisfied, since Plato himself contradicts it in his own writings. For example, in the *Republic* we are told that "imagining" is the poorest form of cognition because it deals with images or mere copies of things we see in the visible world. However, in the same section of the book we find the famous Allegory of the Cave, a most remarkable piece of imaginary writing which is intended to support Plato's epistemic thesis. Again in the *Apology*, Plato has Socrates discredit the wisdom of the poet, because it is based on "inspiration" rather than reason. In the same dialogue we also find Socrates listening to his divine "voice" and referring to himself as a "gadfly" sent to the city of Athens as a gift of God. In spite of his formal protests against poetry, Plato constantly used images to convey his philosophical ideas.

Thus, guided by Plato's own example, the differences between philosophers and poets cannot rest primarily on the fact that one deals with ideas and the other with images.

Writing/Speaking

When Ric tells me he prefers to be a poet speaking than a writer of poems, I am reminded of Socrates' attitude toward writing. Although we are deeply indebted to Plato for his written account of Socrates' life of philosophy, Socrates himself objected to writing his own ideas. One reason for this was Socrates' desire to avoid being considered among the Sophists who wrote speeches to give a display of wisdom. Socrates also thought the written word could do nothing more than remind us of what was already written in our souls. He regarded writing inferior to living discourse because a "written discourse on any subject is bound to contain much that is fanciful." A lover of wisdom who speaks extemporaneously is more a true poet than "one who has nothing to show of more value than the literary works on whose phrases he spends hours, twisting them this way and that, pasting them together and pulling them apart ..."

In Plato's dialogue the *Phaedrus*, Socrates tells us that writing was the invention of an Egyptian god named Theuth. The king of Thebes at that time was Ammon. When Theuth urged Ammon to make use of his invention, the King asked him to explain its value.

"Here, O king," replied Theuth, "is a branch of learning that will make the people of Egypt wiser and improve their memories; my discovery provides a recipe for memory and wisdom." But the king answered and said, "O man full of arts, to one it is given to create the things of art, and to another to judge what measure of harm and of profit they have for those that shall employ them. And so it is that you, by reason of your tender regard for the writing that is your offspring, have declared the very opposite of its true effect. If men learn writing, it will implant forgetfulness in their souls; they will cease to exercise memory because they rely on that which is written, *calling things to remembrance no longer from within themselves, but by means of external marks.*

What you have discovered is a recipe not for memory, but for reminder. And it is no true wisdom that you offer your disciples, but only its semblance, for by telling them of many things without teaching them you will make them seem to know much, while for the most part they know nothing, and as men filled, not with wisdom, but with conceit of wisdom, they will be a burden to their fellows."

In an Author's Note for an earlier book called *Speaking Poems* Ric advises the reader that his poems were written to be heard "somewhere in the morning sun or by a window on a rainy afternoon." "I do not need your analytical mind stopping to measure the weight of these lines; I need your creative spirit flowing to help me free what the printer has locked up here," says Ric. Through the voice of the reader, not only is Ric reincarnated, but the written word is restored to its living form. It seems almost accidental that his poems are printed. When spoken, the words are no longer external marks, but callings to remembrance of ideas, images, and experiences from within ourselves.

Dragons/Dragonflies

One day in a discussion of the differences between philosophers and poets, Ric pointed out to me that few philosophers commit suicide, either slowly or all at once. Poets, on the other hand, are a high risk. A philosopher, Nietzsche said, must "prevent concepts, opinions, things past, and books" to come between himself and what is. Few poets would need this advice. Often they stand in danger of being too close to what is. Frequently they need to gain some distance or establish some "mediation", to use Hegel's term. The poet's problem is to get close enough to his/her dragons to subdue them without getting devoured. From the "Bixby Bridge Incident" poem, written in 1971 (found at the end of this piece), we get the impression that Ric almost "lost it" himself. Reading his recent poems I wouldn't say he has subdued, or made peace with all his dragons, but he seems to be out of immediate danger. Unfortunately, contemporary philosophers, with the exception of Martin Heidegger and a few others, have not been helpful companions for poets, because they think dragons do not exist.

If philosophers generally have little to do with dragons, also they seldom encounter dragonflies. Ric uses the dragonfly to symbolize "the pain and joy of the creative act." Like the poet and the artist, the dragonfly "spends its life both beneath and above the surface of things ... splitting his own skin to emerge, rising up winged and iridescent." Nietzsche, who is both poet and philosopher, chides the Famous Philosophers for their timidity. Using a slightly different image, he says of them, "You are no eagles: so neither do you know the spirit's joy in terror. And he who is not a bird shall not make his home above abysses."

Paradoxes/Contradictions

Ric's poem, "The Paradox as Handled by a Philosopher From a Safe Distance with Mechanical Hands," (found at the end of this piece), suggests that in the realm of paradoxes, philosophers and poets most obviously have taken different paths. A paradox is an assertion seemingly opposed to itself, but, nevertheless, contains a truth. For the poet, paradox is where tragedy and comedy have their origins. Reality itself seems to be paradoxical. It is the poet's joyful pain. (See Ric's "A Poet's Lament" at the end of this piece.) Philosophers, on the other hand, guided by the canon of non-contradiction, have tended to look upon every paradox as a weed to be uprooted. The passion of reason is to resolve paradoxes. Truth must be carefully sorted out from untruth. But, paradoxically, not all contradictions are untrue, even for the philosopher. We find, for example, Socrates ironically admitting that his wisdom consists in knowing that he is not wise. (At this point the paradox should not go unnoticed that I was involved in writing in order to present Socrates's argument on the limitations of writing.) The paradoxical baffles reason in order to show what reason cannot reason. The authors of the Upanishads, the Zen masters, writers like Nietzsche and Kierkegaard, have discovered that the paradoxical is both the spur and the limit of reason. Kierkegaard wrote, "The supreme paradox of all thought is the attempt to discover something that thought cannot think." If reason is offended in this encounter with the paradoxical, than it has nothing to learn.

If, however, it places the love of wisdom *(philo/sophia)* above everything else, reason will welcome poets who are guides to truth in its paradoxical form.

Even as we Speak is a retrospective collection of poems, moving back in time from the present to Ric's first serious poems. In each poem we get a glimpse of what poetry means to Ric Masten. We have heard many difinitions of poetry. Poetry is distilling experience into language. Poetry is making pathways into the "clearing of Being." (Heideggar) Poetry is seeing real toads in an imaginary garden. Poetry may be all of the above, but for Ric it is putting a line of language around an experience that frightens or intrigues us. Ric speaks to us in ideas and images that show us bits of reality that we have forgotten, or have not noticed, or have frightened us off. And, if a paradox can be found anywhere, Ric won't let us pass by without at least noticing it.

Robert O'Brien
Monterey Peninsula College
Monterey, California

THE BIXBY BRIDGE INCIDENT
(From Speaking Poems.)

the cup was half empty
the big hand said forty-two past
and the word if there was one
was tired
then suddenly the wind touched my hair
and i became aware of myself
there on the bridge
a weary old bird ready to leap
from the nest and fly blind
to the breathing sea
     below
me
in my best bulky-knit sweater
calmly inching forward
a great sadness
in my blue gray eyes
     hair blowing
     aware now
i paused and listened to the night
for motor sound
and looked for lights
but the world was empty
no one was coming to witness
     my final scene

        the grand finale
and it was such a fantastic
dramatic moment
i decided to come back
and tell you all about it

laughing
shaking my head
i drove home
but it wasn't until i saw the shape
of my own house
that i realized the cup
had been half full
        all the time

P.S.

i was told recently
that of all witnessed suicides
from the golden gate bridge
in san francisco, california
not one
not a single person
has been seen to go off on the ocean side
the horizon side
all
as of this writing
have been seen leaping back
toward the city
and that would be a hell of a thing
to discover half way down

once years ago
i hung by my heels
was swatted — whaaaaah — and decided
to suck air and live
on a bridge near big sur, california
in the summer of '71
i faced the same decision again

        and as i write this
        i realize
        i am
        three months old today

THE PARADOX AS HANDLED BY A
PHILOSOPHER FROM A SAFE DISTANCE
WITH MECHANICAL HANDS
(From Stark Naked.)

there are those who say
some cases of schizophrenia
may be nothing more than a chemical disorder
and given a day
on something like a dialysis machine
what had appeared to be the cauterized remains

of a dead animal
can now be seen as leg of lamb

at long last
napoleon can take off that silly hat
and go to work in a savings and loan
van gogh can clerk in a shoe store
but what will happen to the poetry
when we are disconnected
from the dream that drives us mad?

some siamese twins are attached in such a way
they can't be separated
and so along with our compulsive drive
toward mental health
let's not forget
that jesus
        managed somehow
knowing he was lord
and at the same time not believing it
an honest to god
flesh and blood
bread and wine
gemini

A POET'S LAMENT
(From Stark Naked.)

the wine i offer up
for communion
was drawn from my own blue vein
     i am that kind of martyr

and when i cough on lillies
the speck of blood is precious
as the hurt of which a child complains
     i am that sorry for myself

at midnight my typewriter
makes the sound
of a blindman's cane
     i am that much in the dark

i speak my poems
with a hand at my brow like olivier
playing the melancholy dane
     i am that despairing

god grant me a storm
that i may once again
walk by your window in the rain
     being that pitiful

you must admit
i cut a tragic figure
but can i say i suffer
     when i so enjoy the pain

PSYCHOLOGY AND A WIZARD

A "Wizard has always been an agent of change, someone who effects us with his personal skill and his sometimes showy style. When Ric Masten is "talking" his work at a party or a convention or a school assembly, about two thirds of the audience appears to see / or / hear / or / feel / the power of his communication. The other third seems to be struggling with feelings of irritation, confusion, embarrassment. They look around furtively. What is going on? Why are these other people so rapt, so moved?

In the field of psychology there is a theory emerging that may partially explain why. Almost everybody has at least five sensory systems that we use to create our experience. If we reason that these senses, connected to our eyes, ears, skins, noses and tongues, bring us sensory data, we can begin to see, / hear / and / feel / some answers. Group our apparatus into the idea of channels of communication, and we can imagine them to be principally visual, auditory or kinesthetic. Input through these systems seems to be shaped, conditioned, switched around and directed by people who are receiving a communication, and by other people who are sending a communication. But — the secret known by "Wizards", the purposeful communicators, the world over and back to forever, is that *no one really operates out of any reality, but only out of his version of it.* "It's a miracle that we communicate at all," Ric says. But, once in a while, someone makes a communication contact with us, someone whose descriptions of joy or pain or sexiness or silliness we can see / hear / or feel are something like our own. The visual, auditory or kinesthetic system that that person is using, makes emotional or symbolic sense to you if it's communicated to you in your system. It makes sense to me it it's my system that is being used. I'm picking up! I'm transcribing! I'm moved. I dance along easily. I can think and feel at the same time. I'm so relaxed as I translate:

I've got it. The world looks, / sounds / or / feels open-ended, exciting and full of choices. I'm being influenced; that is, my description of my experience is. I am affirmed, the feedback is grand. I believe that the communication intended is the communication received. It seems so. Ric says it isn't: that his poems, stories and songs are particulars, not generalizations, that they are about him. But I don't feel / think so, and neither does the part of the audience who are seeing, / hearing / or / feeling their own experience, vividly, through Ric's choices of verbal symbols, movements, changes of voice.

Now, Ric annoys me when he says he doesn't see images in his head, doesn't think in pictures. I can hardly believe him, because I do. But we do seem to have a connection, as I'm discovering my two-thirds of the audience has. I not only see, I also hear ideas and dreams and thoughts and fears and surprises and wonderings and I strongly feel them. Maybe this is where I connect. I usually begin jumping up and down in sync with Ric after a few minutes of listening to his latest. I see the images in his language. They are mine. My experience becomes very personal. But there is another part of me that wants to hear, and to feel a lot of impact. I'm metaphor-hungry. I grew up on elaborate, well-told metaphors and stories, particularly fables and parables, so my nervous system is all ready to learn more about the process of the world in this age-old way. In my metaphors I want statements of likelihoods, not eternal truths. I want paradox. Paradox confuses me, slows me down so that I can absorb a careful summation of what is being said. Some people studying the effect of communication believe that paradox can create trance states in listeners. Whatever happens to me, as a member of the entranced part of the audience, I feel good. I learn and I don't have to do it fast. My mind has noted what has been said, (Ric works in a cognitive overload style: too much to keep track of), and then I have all of "later" to muse and reflect. What Ric has really told me comes to me in an unfolding way, in a state of reverie. Gautama and Socrates and Jesus of Nazareth were clearly outstanding in their use of metaphor. I wonder if I would have understood their communications at the time they were talking to me, if I had experienced those early teachers in the flesh. I have a hunch I might have been looking around wonderingly at the people picking up the messages, looking for the translator, trying to understand the "Wizardry", not knowing it was all inside.

Well, I've got years yet, and Ric to practice on.

Dr. Roberta Richards
Glendale Community College
Glendale, Arizona

A TEACHER LOOKS AT
Ric Masten: One Of Our Failures

Two years ago, Ric Masten was asked to give the keynote address at the annual Arizona English Teacher's Conference in Phoenix. It was a slice of life's irony so rich in lessons for us that I could not resist pointing to it when I introduced him that day. "Ladies and gentlemen," I said to the gathered audience of about four hundred English teachers, "I would like to introduce Ric Masten, one of our failures ..."

Because it was true. Years before, when he was in our English classes in junior high and high school, we failed Ric: with our red pens in our hands and righteousness in our eyes, we told him that he could not write. And on that October afternoon in Phoenix, many years and hundreds of beautiful-meaningful poems later, we were paying him $400 to come back and talk to us for an hour about writing. I would hope that we can learn from that irony—and from the irony of this collection of poetry, written by one of our failures.

Ric Masten is one of our failures in several ways. First, he is one of our failures because we did fail him—we flunked him. We told him that he was dumb and that he could not write. We made him ashamed of his own words; we turned him away from the gift that was in him. Basically, we told him that he could not write because—in his case—he could not spell. And in our smallness, we have often equated spelling (and grammar and punctuation) with the *real* act of language, which is deep and complex and powerful far beyond these small acts of editing. And so we flunked Ric Masten—and millions of others like him before and since.

But Ric was not dumb (nor have the other millions been). In Ric's case, he suffered (largely because we chose to make him suffer) from dyslexia—"neurological impairment of the ability to read." But listen to what Marilyn Ferguson tells us (in *The Aquarian Conspiracy*) about dyslexia:

Dyslexia, which afflicts at least 10 percent of the population, seems to be associated with a dominance by the right cerebral hemisphere in the reading process. Those with a strong holistic perception are often handicapped by our educational system with its emphasis on symbolic language and symbolic mathematics. They have initial difficulty in processing these symbols. Yet this neurological minority may also be unusually gifted. They typically excel in the arts and in innovative thinking. Ironically, their potential contribution to society is frequently diminished because the system undermines their self-esteem in their first school years (p.299).

As the blind high priests of language, we could not see this. We could only see misspelled words. And so, we took (or tried to take) the gift of language away from Ric Masten.

Ric, then, is one of our failures in another way: we failed him. We failed to help him—because of our own blindness—to see and nurture and develop the gift of language that was in him even then. We did not have to see or believe that he would become a published poet—few of our students will do that. But we did need to see and believe that the gift of language—as a tool for psychological and spiritual survival—was in him then. Because it was. As it is in all of us, whether or not we can spell.

I wrote a poem myself once, a poem about the grimness of this left-brained blindness in our education, a poem about a small boy on his way to school one morning ...

Along the road to the gray stone school,
he found a ragged butterfly
blazing out its life beside a pool
of last night's autumn rain
(the wind had brought a crimson leaf to lie
beside the yellow butterfly);
all this was wrapped with music in his mind—
but then from the gray stone school
the indifferent bell summoned him to find
death of quite another kind.

And so it has been all too often in our schools. And so it was with Ric. But in his case, there is good news in spite of all this—because he is one of our failures in yet another way. Ric is also one of our failures because he failed to believe us when we told him he was dumb and because he failed to let us take his language away from him. You see, Ric was just mean and stubborn enough that he wouldn't quite buy what we told him back then. Granted, it took him a while, but eventually he found out what real language was all about. And when he did, his "giftedness" began to emerge; and he began to write poetry that touched people and that spoke to them beneath the surface of their lives.

The turning point came when Ric made that same discovery about language that Eldridge Cleaver made while he was in Folsom Prison—that writing is so much more than a matter of spelling and punctuation. Cleaver says it in those few powerful words from *Soul On Ice:* "That is why I started to write. To save myself." And William Stafford, another poet, speaks of that same crucial insight about language when he has the muse in one of his poems speak these words: "When / you allow me to live with you, every / glance at the world around you will be / a sort of salvation."

In spite of the lack of help from us, Ric Masten eventually found his muse. He discovered by himself what his language was for—and he set about using it to save himself. That is what this collection is all about. That is, as Ric himself will tell you, what all his poetry is about. And saving oneself has little to do with spelling and commas and semicolons; rather, it has to do with saying one's feelings. Or, in Ric's own words, "putting a corral of words around the stuff that's in our gut and our heart."

Follow this book back from the end (which is the beginning) to the beginning (which is now), and you will sense the turning point and you will see the change. You will feel the moment when Ric discovers the gift of his words— and his words become gifts to us.

So, I am glad that Ric is one of our failures in this third sense. I am glad that he now goes about the country undoing for others what was done to him. I am glad that he gives his gift so freely. He teaches us well. And in our gray stone schools, I hope that we who profess to teach writing are at last beginning to learn the lesson of this poet who is one of our failures.

G. Lynn Nelson
Arizona State
Tempe, Arizona

102

BOOKS

Also available on order, through local bookstores that use R. R. Bowker Company BOOKS IN PRINT catalogue system

☐ EVEN AS WE SPEAK by Ric Masten. **Paperback $5.50**
   112 pages. ISBN 0-931104-12-2

☐ the DESERTED ROOSTER by Ric Masten. **Paperback $5.00**
   96 pages. ISBN 0-931104-11-4

☐ STARK NAKED by Ric Masten. **☐ Paperback $4.95**
   110 pages. ISBN 0-931104-04-1 **☐ Hardcover $9.95**

☐ VOICE OF THE HIVE by Ric Masten. **Paperback $4.95**
   104 pages. ISBN 0-931104-02-5

☐ SPEAKING POEMS by Ric Masten. **Paperback $4.95**
   112 pages. ISBN 0-931104-06-8

☐ HIS & HERS by Ric & Billie Masten. **Paperback $3.95**
   80 pages. ISBN 0-931104-01-7

☐ OWNING THE BEAST AND THE BAD GIRL **Paperback $3.50**
   by Billie Barbara Masten.
   40 pages. ISBN 0-931104-07-6

RECORD ALBUM

☐ Ric Masten Singing **Price $5.50**
   LET IT BE A DANCE
   12 Songs. Stereo SF-1002

BROADSIDES . . . Price .50

Single sheets printed on colored stock. 8½"x11", suitable for framing.

☐ The Warty Frog   ☐ Let It Be a Dance
☐ The Second Half   ☐ The Homesick Snail

PUBLICITY PAMPHLETS

☐ Ric Masten in Concert . . . ☐ On the College Campus.
☐ In the High School . . . ☐ In the Middle School.
☐ In the Elementary . . . ☐ In the Church . . . ☐ On Relationships.
☐ Honorarium and Fee Schedule.

....

CHECKS MADE OUT TO

SUNFLOWER INK
Palo Colorado Canyon
Carmel, CA 93923

ORDER $ _____

6% SALES TAX (CA. RES.) _____

SHIPPING & HANDLING $ __$1.00__

TOTAL $ _____

Name _____

Address _____

City _____ State _____ Zip _____